This Black Girl's Diary

Inspirational Self-Guided Journal

By Natia Nichole

Foreword: To every young woman who will face the toughest challenge, LIFE.

Dedication

In memory of my grandmother Adele; a woman of class and prestige! Her goal in life was to make every woman feel invincible. She strived to instill self- esteem, empowerment, and nobility in all women.

To Dominique, my beautiful cousin who never had the chance to bloom, this is for you.

To my father Donnell, I would not be who I am today without your life's sacrifice. May you rest in power.

To all of the women who have jumped through hurdles to get where you are today and shared those experiences with the future generation of women, thank you.

Mom, you know what it is.

My queen, I love you.

Table of contents:

First, get to know the woman who is going to have you write the very details of your life down that will mold you into a powerful woman. Yes, I am about to be all up in your business.

I am Natia Nichole and I grew up in York, PA better known as Y.C. I used to be ashamed of this place, but as I grew; I took great pride in the city that has made me who I am today. A city full of beauty and brains with many talents. I grew up the way many young girls grow up; fatherless, teen mother, inner city school living in an economically disadvantaged neighborhood.

My grandma was the head of the household, church was required on Sundays and prayer was a must. Not sure if many young parents make their kids go to church anymore. It is sad, because I do believe that was one force that has helped me become who I am. Ahhh but yes, I prevailed and right after high school I went to the first black degree granting institution: Lincoln University of Pennsylvania. I'm a proud HBCU graduate. I majored in English Education and became an impeccable educator.

After receiving my degree, I returned to my hometown and taught at my alma-mater to jog my career. A few years later, I fasted, prayed and received a sign to move to Charlotte, NC; this is where I taught Senior English for five years. Charlotte is where I met some of the best mentors and friends. In 2020, in the midst of the Covid Pandemic I relocated to Houston, Texas, with my two dogs. I started to develop my seven streams of income, pursue a master's degree and make God a priority. Here I am today, praying my share of experiences through this diary allows you to overcome pain and envision a better future. My life revolves around the beauty of existence, a gift from God. Working with people is my passion; it allows me to share my joy and dreams in hopes of helping other women find their aspirations. I hope to be a prime example of what any young woman can achieve. I have been through the storm, and I am the rainbow that shines brightly after.

Hello beautiful,

I started writing at the tender age of 4. My grandmother tells the story all the time about how I used to fall asleep with a pencil in my hand, held to paper at the kitchen table. When I was younger, I fell in love with being able to express myself through writing. Writing isn't just words on a piece of paper, but it's our feelings, emotions, and ideas. Once recorded these things are given life, breath, and existence. Writing allows you to be you with no interruptions, it allows you to be creative, and that is what gives you "life." Writing isn't just about grammar and punctuation, but about painting images, allowing yourself to see through words, a form of self-rehabilitation. I wrote my father's killer 13 letters over the course of two years and never sent one. As I looked back at each piece of writing it was obvious my heart had shifted. The more letters I wrote the more I forgave him; written therapy is what I called it. It was then I realized how much writing something down can change your mindset. I write everything down from tasks, to goals, notes, stories, quotes and journal entries; all of which have helped me master life as a black woman.

There is power in writing! You're never too old to keep a diary.

I'm a black girl in America.

This is my story.

-Natia Nichole-

Entry 1
A Young Mother's Love:

Having a baby at a young age may seem cool but...

My mother got pregnant at the tender age of 15, too young of a girl to raise another; she did her absolute best. Every year I reflect on what has made me a woman, and at 15 I'm sure the only factor that made my mother a woman was becoming a mother herself. Body still maturing, hair still trying to figure out all the places to grow, and the mind still developing. There was a lack of life experiences on her part, untamed emotions, growth mindset, stunted because her life was no longer hers, it was mine. I was her baby; she loved me, and I was super cute. She was perfect in my eyes. My mother did her best, but I struggled anyway because my father didn't do his part. There were times I wish she had chosen a better dad for me. There were so many things in life my mother could not teach me because she was still learning herself. She couldn't teach me about finances because we were living with her mother, she couldn't teach me about boys because she didn't even know herself yet, and she couldn't teach me all there was to know about God because he was still working on her. So, there I was born with the shortest head start one could have, which indeed was no head start at all. However, I did have love and that's what got me where I am today. Have you considered how much your mother or provider loves you despite their shortcomings? Stop being selfish for a moment and think of how many times someone who loves you has gone without so you could have it all.

"

Be thankful for what you have; you'll end up having more. If you concentrate on what you don't have, you will never, ever have enough."

~Oprah Winfrey~

How old was your mother/father when you were conceived?

____

What's one thing your mother/father could improve on to make your life more manageable?

____

What will you do differently than your parents?

____

Tell me about your mother and/or father.

____
____
____
____
____
____
____
____
____
____
____
____
____
____

Entry 2
Inmate
BQ – 2311

More often than not, minorities disproportionately lose their loved ones to the prison systems. That's a whole other conversation, just know it has impacted me as well, and maybe you too.

BQ-2311 was my father's inmate number. I learned that before I even knew his entire name. My father spent most of my life in prison. Each and every one of my birthday celebrations my secret wish was always for my father to be there. I loved him more than anything, it was his spirit I was attracted to. His smile I would gaze at all day long when visiting the penitentiary. He gave me butterflies. I felt like a princess in his arms, the visits were conjugal, so I was able to feel the warmth of his love. My mom allowed me to believe that one day there would be change; she never mentioned how heart- breaking that change could be.

Often young teenage girls are forced to grow up without fathers. Young girls are turning into products of their environment. Makes me wonder, does a father not know his importance, or has America painted the black man as a monster that we started to believe in? Black men are given less opportunity than any other race on this planet. Furthermore, the most harm being done is to young black girls like myself. Nevertheless, the Black woman will always find ways to adapt. The Black woman; a strong, prominent figure.

"I am not free while any woman is unfree, even when her shackles are very different from my own."

—Audre Lorde

Do you know anyone in prison or have a friend who does? How has that impacted you or them? Does this person's absence affect your life? If so, how and why or why not?

Entry 3
Unprotected

She would wait until the lights were dim and everyone was asleep. There we lay in the dark on her full-sized bed. I always knew at any moment she would roll over and climb on top of me. I never said anything, I just laid there. I knew telling would cause an uproar. There was a weird part of me that enjoyed the affection but hated how and who it was coming from. Many often think of abuse as someone older making sexual contact with a minor, but abuse comes in all ages and sizes. When I was younger my grandmother used to take me to her friend's house to play with her daughters, they were church going folks, so they had to be ok right? I was the same age as the girl who would hump me at night, possibly 10 or 11. She was way bigger than me and physically threatening, so there I would lay as she assaulted me. My dad was in prison so he couldn't protect me. I think back now and wonder "Did she know better?" We were the same age, but I eventually came to the conclusion that someone didn't protect her either. As a result, behaviors triggered in me that I found hard to forgive myself for. How could I be in a house of the Lord and still be in danger. It was then I started to lose my faith. In my eyes there couldn't be a God.

"My mission in life is not merely to survive, but to thrive; and to do so with some passion, some compassion, some humor, and some style."

-Maya Angelou-

Have you ever felt unprotected? Share those thoughts in hopes of healing.

Entry 4
The Worst Phone Call Ever

It was a hot summer night as thunderstorms and bolts of lightning cracked in the sky. I was unable to sleep as the limbs from the trees began to sway and the night grew darker and more terrifying. I tossed and turned trying to ignore the storm that I knew was coming, but it was inevitable. I had this feeling in my body something was going to happen, and it wasn't a good thing. Have you ever experienced your intuition? Sis, let me tell you my gut feeling that night was stronger than I ever experienced. As I squeezed my pillow tighter the loud roaring cracks of lightning grew. I could feel it in my soul something bad was going to happen, so I laid and awaited the inevitable. I closed my eyes and tried to think of something positive. As I laid there I thought to myself. When I was younger people used to say that God was working on something or that he was angry when it stormed. Others looked at it as an act of Mother Nature. Immediately interrupting my thoughts my cell phone rang; it was my mother, the news she gave me shoved bolts of lightning through my body and my heart stopped. I will never forget those words and the empathetic tone in her voice.

"Your father has been killed."

At that moment, all I could think of was how am I going to manage life as a fatherless girl!

So many thoughts ran through my mind. I screamed because I could not find the words to say anything else. I questioned God. Why did the Lord forsake me now?

"We delight in the beauty of the butterfly, but rarely admit the changes it has gone through to achieve that beauty"

Maya Angelou

Have you lost someone dear to your heart? Who was/is that person? ___________________________

How will this person's absence impact your life journey? When the time comes how will you fill that void?

____
____
____
____
____
____
____
____
____
____
____
____
____
____
____
____
____
____
____
____
____
____
____

Entry 5
Fatherless

Simply put, my father was murdered. The first man we look up to as women is our fathers. There is something special about the father daughter bond. My dad was exactly what I wanted in a man at one point; sounds crazy right, I know. My father made me smile, he gave me butterflies, he called me his princess, and reminded me of how beautiful I was all the time. It was his goal to protect me until he didn't. My father's absence made room for all of the other heart breaks I've encountered, despite the many times my heart has been broken by others, the reality is my own father broke it first. Deep inside I wanted a father but when I dug a little deeper, I knew he could never be. It started with his consistent absences at any major event in my life due to incarceration. The reality is, he is dead now. Even before being killed, drug abuse stole his soul and prison was his first home.

I remember where it all started.

Every year my mother would have huge birthday celebrations for me, and I would get what any girl would've thought were the best gifts in the world. I collected tons of dolls, kitchenettes, Nano babies, and handheld electronic video games. Most of the time the only thing I ever wanted as a gift was for my father to be present for at least one birthday party. My father never made it to any of my birthday parties growing up, but I will always remember the one and only birthday gift I received. He was released one day from prison, and he purchased my very first baby blue pager. I remember like it was yesterday because everyone had pagers back in 2003. You're probably wondering how old I am but trust me everyone had a pager. I remember like it was yesterday, my father and I went to the store and picked out the one I liked most, you couldn't tell me anything about my dad that day; he was the best dad ever. That was until he returned to prison before the first bill was due and just like that; my beloved gift was gone. I still carried the physical remnants because it was symbolic. It was a symbol of my father's love for me. And, to think he said he would buy my first new car once I graduated college. (Imagine that).

It was during that time my heart started to deteriorate and those moments I wished I had a father figure no longer existed; he broke my heart. My next heartbreak was given to me by a young man that I swore I loved. I wanted him to tell me how beautiful I was and how special I was just as my father used to tell me. One thing for certain I knew if I had my father's love that young man's love wouldn't have been able to penetrate my heart. Of course, my mother told me how beautiful I was and how much I didn't need that boy, but when you're young you don't want to hear that crap. Mothers always know best, just know later in life you will understand her decisions. Unfortunately, until then you will hold her accountable for your poor actions.

My heart struggled to repair itself from the millions of tiny pieces caused by the impact. It was at that moment I knew the father/daughter relationship that I had longed for my entire life was no longer possible. You may be reading this and thinking "well I have a father." If you have a dad, it is truly a blessing, but maybe someone else is missing that could have changed your life for the better. Anyone come to mind?

Although I like to think I'm healing, my father will continue to break my heart for the rest of my life. He won't be there to walk me down the aisle and he will miss important moments with his future grandchildren, moments every girl dreams of having her father be a part of. The unintentional pain my father has inflicted on me is a forever pain. Have you ever felt eternal pain? There's no medication for that, only GOD. Trust me I know how hard it is to find God after tragedy, but I promise it is all worth it. It is so important to believe because without it, life becomes even more unbearable. Believing allows you to survive. I grew up in a Christian home but truly didn't find God until I was mature enough to open my own heart. Through all of the heartbreak there is healing and that helps you to become the person you're destined to be, but first you must allow yourself to be in a state of healing. I found God and what works for me may not work for you but finding something is key. I found God and he assured me that if my father was still alive today, I would not be where I am, such a tough pill to swallow.

In fact, my father's death has allowed me to move forward as a healer for others, my purpose. Please go to church if you can. I had been forced for many years to attend a church every Sunday where I swore the preacher was spitting on the mic and speaking another language, but the more mature I grew, the easier it was for me to find a church home. I felt the word was being spoken to me directly. Study the books of the bible and you will see, your life aligns a lot more than you know.

Nevertheless, my father's death paid his debt to society. Through his mistakes I was left here to leave a lasting impact on the lives of others. That is my superpower and I consider myself a super-hero. So in the end or maybe just the beginning I found a new relationship with God. I now know my father died for me to become the woman I am today. The biggest sacrifice any man could give a daughter. The greatest gift accompanied by a broken heart. If you're living with a broken heart, it is time to mend it.

Challenges Make You Discover Things About Yourself You Never Really Knew

Cicely Tyson

Is there someone (dead or alive) you wish(ed) you could have a relationship with? What is so special about this person? Talk to me!

Entry 6
Tragedy

I've been told when people die they go in 3's. May or may not be true but it seems so in my case. In 2008 shortly after my father's death in 2007, I would have never guessed I would lose 3 people that year. Senior week was the week before graduation in college and we were sitting on the bus headed to the Philadelphia Laff House Comedy club. We were on the yellow buses about to pull off and just before doing so my mother called again. This time my great- grandmother passed away. She was in her 90's but it hurt so bad because she was the wisdom I've always had in my life. She had a stroke and as fast as I could, I hopped off of the bus, hopped in my car and drove home to York, PA. Just like that she was gone. I learned so much from her. If you still have your grandparents sit down and ask them about their lives and experiences. I learned so much from my grandmother, including the details on my slave given last name.

About 4 weeks later my mom's nephew, my cousin committed suicide and weeks later his father, my mom's brother died in his 30's from Cancer. I share these deaths with you because as you grow, those around you will move on to another life; some you were close to and some maybe not so much. Death increases rapidly as life grows older and your senses become more heightened. Storms in life are inevitable, but the question is how will you handle them? How would you deal with the loss of your father, mother, grandparents, siblings, aunts, uncles, or even close friends?

"There is no force equal to a woman determined to rise"

W.E.B Dubois~

How mentally prepared are you to deal with losing multiple people you love?

Who would it hurt to lose the most, and why?

Entry 7
Insecurities

There were parts of me I couldn't stand. I never wore shorts because of a condition known as Folliculitis (Ingrown Hair Follicles) A black girl's skin requires special care. My mom tried a few times to heal the wounds of my heart due to my skin issues. I never wanted to wear shorts because my skin reminded me of shedded snake skin. Eventually my skin healed but it was definitely on God's time. Then to top it all off I had Eczema, every black girl's nightmare. The insecurities didn't stop there. I hated my hair. It was so long and healthy (something I didn't realize until reflecting) but its thickness made me sick; my mother tried to fix that also, but *"Just for Me"* perms only made my hair fall out. Not to mention my teeth were crooked and to make matters worse I had no father to remind me of my beauty (Yes, this fatherless thing really took a toll on my soul). My mother always told me I was beautiful, but I wanted to hear it from him. We all have insecurities but what many people forget to teach is that those same insecurities grow into the very special features that make you who you are. When I post pictures on social media and people comment "It's the legs for me," "It's the dimples for me," "It's the locs for me," "It's the complexion for me." I never knew my features that would stand out the most were those very same features I hated as a child. Trust the process.

(Adj.) Flawsome
An individual who embraces their "Flaws" and knows they are awesome regardless.

-Marilyn Monroe-

What insecurities do you face? What about them makes you uncomfortable?

Entry 8
Sex

Do you know what insecurities lead to… you guessed it SEX!

As I walked into the building people yelled "Don't Kill Me Mommy," "You're a murderer." They held signs and protested outside the very same clinic I was about to enter. The most painful part about the abortion was not the procedure itself but that I was alone, just as I felt I had been my entire life. After having my finger pricked, I was sent to sit in a waiting room. As I looked around, I realized each and every one of us waiting was there for the same thing; we all wore band aids on our pinky fingers where blood was drawn. We were all there to abort God's gift. One I knew of as sin.

There I was again unprotected. It was crazy because my partner and I used protection, but the condom broke and of course with my luck, I became pregnant. A freshman in college who was about to experience abortion. Sex didn't just expose me to an unknown world, it literally took over my world. I only had one partner at the time, but sex became the norm for us when pregnancy number 2 occurred shortly after, and again I went to the clinic. Sex became my way of receiving intimacy, too young to experience an orgasm but rather the introduction of feeling, and what it felt like to be loved by a man since my father was to no avail.

My mother gave me "The Talk" far too late. I was already sexually active by the age of 15. I grew to think loving a man required giving him my goods and for him to love me in return; I was expected to lay on my back. I had also watched this from the many porn flicks I snuck and watched at a friend's house. I had no business hanging with that friend; she's part of the reason I had that itch to have intercourse in the first place. Please watch who you surround yourself with. That old saying you're the company you keep is the realist statement ever. Friends around me began to put their trust in these boys and pregnancy was the usual result, but there were a few who were given STDs that were hard to shake.

My world was "Boys, boys, boys." Everything I did I wanted to look cute for the "boys." If this is you please find something else to entertain yourself with. The "boys" will use you and leave you because most of them just don't know any better.

Know your worth

"You're your best thing"

-Toni Morrison-

"You wanna fly... you've got to give up all the shit weighing you down."

-Toni Morrison

As a young woman how does over-sexualization impact your life? Are you infatuated with social media? Instagram and TikTok are like resumes now. What would someone say about your page if they saw it?

Entry 9
Nightmares

As if my life wasn't already a tough one, those same traumas from my past began to impact my sleep. I dreamt of my aborted babies growing older, I dreamt of my father; headless carrying his head in a trash bag; I called these nightmares. I started sleeping with the TV on because it was only in silence did my dreams crossover from good to bad. The static noise from the TV helped me sleep. It was as if the devil wouldn't give up. Sleeping with white noise avoided the nightmares until one day walking to my car I stopped in my tracks. My nightmares were no longer just vivid pictures in my head at bedtime, they were walking, living, and breathing. I looked around the parking lot and to my surprise there was no one else around. I knew this scent all too well; it was my father's cologne. It was as if he had just walked past me, lingered for a few seconds and then kept moving. Instantly I had an anxiety attack in the middle of the parking lot. I couldn't seem to catch my breath until God gave me a second wind. My dreams were becoming reality.

"It does not do to dwell on dreams and forget to live."

— J.K. Rowling, Harry Potter and the Sorcerer's Stone

What is the worst dream you ever had? How real was it? What would you do if that dream re-occurred often?

Entry 10
Vices
Smoking

I think my friends thought I smoked because I found it to be cool. Nah, I smoked because I saw my father doing it. It was like a trance; I would smoke and feel like I was close to him. I'm sure there is some psychological term for this but to me it was spending time with my father. I didn't smoke until he died. He would stand out back and smoke Black & Milds all the time when he was home, and I would watch in the distance. I had believed his spirit still lingered so I started going out back to smoke also. I just knew we were there together. It wasn't the feelings I got from smoking; it was the memories it brought back; the ones I wanted to relive. Black and Milds eventually became marijuana. I'm not proud of it but this is my story. I'm sharing my story in hopes to make a difference to yours. By the grace of God, I never tried anything "Hardcore" as one would describe it, but it could have easily happened. There are quite a few girls from high school who are addicted to drugs. I used cigars and weed to cope with life.

"Only a Fool Would Put His Lips at the End of a Burning Fire"

-Unknown-

What are your vices? How did they start and how do you plan to stop them?

Entry 11
How I learned what Love Looks Like

We will be wrapping it up here soon, but I shared most of my life with you in hopes you learn from my mistakes. Over the course of my life, I have become a phenomenal woman due to the many different women in my life. My mother had me young, so I was able to watch all of my grandparents take on life and do it well.

Growing up I was blessed with an abundance of grandparents. I was able to meet two of my great grandmothers and they were alive most of my life. I didn't lose them until I was a college graduate. Both great grandmothers were from my maternal side. My grandmothers were beautiful women.

I was fortunate to grow up with multiple grandparents due to divorce and the addition of "step" grandparents. Often in life we tend to forget the significance of our grandparents. We aren't fully mature enough to appreciate their presence until it's too late. If you currently have your grandparents, please sit them down and get to know them. Learning more about them is learning more about yourself.

I had decided to do that one day and the origin of my last name was confirmed. Although I already knew my name was not one of my ancestors, I was told the story from my great grandmother about how her grandparents were slaves on the Palmer Plantation. My name is Natia Palmer and to hear those words come from her mouth inspired me to no longer pass down "my" last name to my children. I now have wisdom.

Grandparents have experienced things beyond our wildest imagination. They carry the knowledge and wisdom to guide future generations and yet we let them pass on to the next life without learning anything from them.

I learned that in order to become the best version of myself; I must know where I come from.

I come from strong women where family is everything. In order to start a beautiful legacy of my own I must follow in my grandmothers' footsteps.

I want to love my husband as much as my grandmothers loved theirs.

I want to experience the same emotions and feelings that I was able to observe throughout my childhood.

This is how I learned what love looks like.

What made me write this blog was the recent death of my grandfather Rick Powell.

(3/08/2020).

I spoke with my grandmother that day and I said to her,

"I am glad you're not alone."

"I feel better knowing there's a house full of people to mourn with you."

Her response was one of compassion and discomfort. It was the saddest thing I have ever heard a woman say.

She said,

"Although there are so many people here to comfort me on the outside, I'm very much alone on the inside."

It was a strange feeling for me to interpret. I wasn't sure how to feel. I was somewhere between admiration for how much she loved her husband and heartbroken because she would never have him again. It was at that moment I knew I wanted to love a man the exact way all of my grandmothers loved theirs.

Ladies, it's important to love a man the correct way but it is also important for him to make you want to love him unconditionally, my grandfathers did that for my grandmothers.

Rick and Cassaundra Powell (Maternal grandparents: My mom's mother and stepfather).

Cassaundra was and still is a devoted Christian woman, my grandfather not so much but they managed to survive. Their relationship has taught me the importance of sacrifice. It has taught me that I cannot expect a man to be exactly who I think he should be, but it is imperative to let him be his individual self. My pop pop Rick played an intricate role in my upbringing. He was my best friend at heart, he played with me when I had no friends, and his job was tough because I was an only child, which left it up to him to entertain me for hours and hours. My grandmother raised me in the church and for that I thank her. Attending church has made me the woman I am today. There are many young people who aren't being raised in the church anymore. Despite what many believe set the foundation for Christianity, it has taught me the values and morals that I believe are important for everyone to learn. My grandma instilled qualities in me that she learned from reading the books of the bible. She taught me that anything I wanted I could get, anything I aspired to be, I could be, and anything I dreamed of becoming could come true; all by the grace of God. She taught me scriptures and prayers and she read books to me every night. She is the reason I've become a teacher. I learned how to love life from her. I am who I am today because of my grandmother. Relationship wise she has taught me that no two people are the same and in order for a marriage to last and be enjoyable both must be committed and willing to sacrifice, add a little bit of prayer on top of that and things will become more clear. It was then I learned what unconditional love is.

R.I.H Pop Rick

John and Ruthie Palmer (Maternal Grandparents: My mom's dad and stepmother.)

I didn't have much of a relationship with Ruth growing up, but we started to build once I was in high school. It was then that I realized I've been missing out on a relationship with one of the most beautiful souls I have ever met. Ruth lost my grandfather John a few years back and although the journey has been a tough one, I can't say my reflection of their past doesn't make me smile. Grandma Ruth catered to my grandfather, and she was devoted to him, something I admired. She took care of this man day in and day out and I remember looking at her thinking

"I want to be as great of a wife as she is."

He would watch her cater to him with a look of gratitude. My grandfather was a vet, and her service was deemed honorable to him. He would watch movies in his recliner and she would bring him breakfast, lunch, and dinner served on a silver platter. I learned what love was from her. I am who I am today because of my grandmother. I learned how to serve a man through her actions.

R.I.H Pop Pop John

Judson & Barbara Denson (Paternal Grandparents: My father's parents).

Barbara, my Nanna, is one of my best friends. Judson & Barb did whatever they could to make sure their grand kids were well taken care of. My grandparents have been together for more than 30 years. My pop pop taught me how I should be treated, and my Nanna taught me how to be strong and fierce. They taught me what a marriage should look like. My Nanna took care of the home and my pop took care of us all. They were like Bonnie & Clyde except my pop pop was Bonnie and my Nanna was Clyde. My Nanna was the strong independent woman, and my pop pop was the calm & collective one; down for whatever in the relationship. I love their relationship. It was always a good time at pop & nan's house. There was always laughter and jokes coming from this household, something we all needed in life. They made me forget my father wasn't present. I learned from her that love, laughter, and forgiveness is important. My Nanna has a beautiful soul and takes pride in who she is. I learned what love is through her. I am who I am today because of my Nanna.

Lester & Jean Mary Bryant aka Granny Panties. (My stepfather's mom & Dad).

I never had the opportunity to meet Pop pop Lester, but Jean was always enough. I was blessed to have her come into my life at the tender age of 4. She would watch movies with me over and over and over again. She treated me as if I was hers and just as excited as I was to see my "blood" grandparents. I was just as happy to see her; we share a special bond. I call her my rollie because she will sit in the passenger seat and ride til the wheels fall off without ever complaining. Growing up she had a few sweethearts here and there but no one that I really saw too often with my own eyes. I knew she dated but out of respect for her late husband she kept most men at a distance. Grannie made sure her grands knew who was pop pop; even in the grave she respected this man, I desire to love someone that much. She taught me how important loyalty is. I learned from her to be honest and to do so tastefully. I learned from her to cherish my future husband. I am who I am today because of my Grannie Panties.

R.I.H Pop pop Lester. Thank you for your son.

I desire to be the same grandma to my grandkids as my grandparents were to me.

Today, I am a combination of these four women. Grandmothers play such an important role in our lives. Having them to cherish is important. One day I'm going to make my mom a grandmother with a relationship that reflects hers as well as my grandparents. If you know me then you know I withhold every characteristic that these women have,

All in one. I'm blessed.

"As you grow older you will learn you have two hands, one for helping yourself and one for helping others."

-Maya Angelou-

My question to you is how will you know what's real love and what's not? Who are some relatives you are blessed to have?

Entry 12
Finding Faith and Defining Success

As I entered the church doors the pastor was giving his sermon. As I approached the pew, he stopped in the midst of his preaching and asked to pray for me. I told him sure, I mean who couldn't use some extra support.

He prayed: "Father, let her know you have not forsaken her."

"Let her know you see her and prove her doubt in your existence to be false."

"Allow her to hear you speak."

That Sunday I left church a different person.

My vision became clear. My mother's young love making allowed me to have two moms; a blessing; my grandmother and my mother.

My father's very absence due to his drug addiction kept him from harming my life even more.

My father's death put an end to a dream that I would have always chased if he were still alive; the dream of being a girl with a father.

BQ2311 made me a better writer, communicator, and teacher. I'm more relatable to all my students than I could ever imagine.

The sexual abuse helps me help other young women alike.

I've learned there is no other guarantee in life but death.

I've learned your insecurities can become your greatest assets

I've learned sex can lead you to a very dark place.

Most importantly GOD is always with you even when you can't see clearly.

Faith & Fear can't exist together!

"I don't like to gamble, but if there's one thing I'm willing to bet on, it's myself."

Beyonce Knowles~

How do you plan to prevent life's obstacles from weighing you down?

Entry 13
The Importance of Goal Setting

For many years I never truly knew what it meant to set goals for myself or how to achieve them. I'm not even sure I knew what a goal was, of course I knew the definition but applying it to my life was something I was unsure of.

How could I implement goals into my life when I wasn't even sure who I was as a woman? In fact, I'm still not 100% sure, but for the first time in my 33 years of living I have felt myself growing spiritually and mentally. It took me 33 years to finally plant seeds that started to bloom before the season changed. These seeds were waiting on me, your seeds are waiting on you. We all have the seeds in our reach, but the soil must be fertile before planting. What I mean by that is your goals won't grow unless you do.

I believe it's ok to still be figuring out life at the age of 34. Many women are rushed in life by parents, friends, and society. My family always tells me "When are you going to have a baby?" My friends always say "Where's your man? "And society (social media) constantly tells me that I am so far behind financially. Once I came to the realization that it's absolutely ok to be where I am in life, that's when things began to change. Be you and only you. There will always be something you want that you can't currently have, there will always be someone prettier than you, and there will always be some sort of rhetoric from society that implies that your life sucks. I consider myself a Sunflower, but I have yet to grow all of my petals because I am still blooming. One day I will fully bloom, and I know that because I have finally planted the seeds to do so. This year I plan to add a little sun to my shine and more petals to my sunflower.

Every year as women we need to set goals for ourselves, and they should be realistic. I used to set unrealistic goals for myself, and I never conquered them. This year I broke those goals down into smaller components. I decided to start this new year off with a theme, one that would help me achieve my goals, one to live by. My theme this year is “keys.” It is my intent to achieve new keys to every door in my life. My first set of keys will be to my new ride, my second set of keys will be to my new apartment, my third set of keys will be to my new classroom, and my fourth set will hopefully be me giving the key to my heart to a very deserving young man. These goals may seem hefty, but my plans are so minuscule that there's no way they won’t happen. God has opened up a new door in my life, the door of wisdom, knowledge and confidence. I plan to use those very same keys to open more doors.

Set a theme for your new beginnings. Just a little sun can go a long way. So, I ask how will you add a little sun to your shine? Make it your time.

-Natia Nichole-

Step by Step what's your 5-year plan?

How do you intend to live life differently after completing your journal?

Before I go,

I want you to know how powerful you are, how smart you are, how beautiful you are, and how important you are. Everyone has a purpose; each stop along your journey is meaningful. Embrace struggle, endure pain, and proceed to success.

I love you truly,

Natia Nichole

www.ingramcontent.com/pod-product-compliance
Lightning Source LLC
LaVergne TN
LVHW010543100826
845148LV00013B/2583

* 9 7 8 0 5 7 8 3 5 6 7 7 8 *